Eat Right

Tips for Good Nutrition

by Katie Bagley

Consultant:
Joan Bushman, MPH, RD
American Dietetic Association

Bridgestone Books

an imprint of Capstone Press
Mankato, Minnesota

Bridgestone Books are published by Capstone Press
151 Good Counsel Drive, P.O. Box 669, Mankato, Minnesota 56002
http://www.capstone-press.com

Library of Congress Cataloging-in-Publication Data
Bagley, Katie.
    Eat right: tips for good nutrition/by Katie S. Bagley.
    p. cm.—(Tips for good nutrition) (Your health)
    Includes bibliographical references and index.
    ISBN 0-7368-0971-6
    1. Nutrition—Juvenile literature. 2. Food—Juvenile literature. [1. Nutrition.] I. Title.
II. Series. III. Series: Your health
TX355 .B35 2002
613.2—dc21   00-012535

Summary: An introduction to the benefits of good nutrition, including the Food Guide Pyramid, vitamins, minerals, proteins, and fats.

Editorial Credits
Sarah Lynn Schuette, editor; Karen Risch, product planning editor; Linda Clavel, designer
    and illustrator

Photo Credits
Artville, 6 (insets)
Capstone Press/Gary Sundermeyer, 6 (insets), 16
Comstock, Inc., 4, 8, 10
Gregg R. Andersen, cover, 12, 14, 18, 20
PhotoDisc, Inc., 1

**Bridgestone Books thanks Mari Schuh and Franklin Elementary School, Mankato, Minnesota, for
providing photo shoot locations.**

09/02

2 3 4 5 6 07 06 05 04 03 02

Table of Contents

Good Nutrition

Good nutrition is important to your health. Eating the right foods gives you energy. Your body needs proteins, carbohydrates, fats, vitamins, minerals, and water. These nutrients help you think, grow, and play.

nutrient
something that is needed by people, animals, and plants to stay strong and healthy

The Food Guide Pyramid

Fats, Oils and Sweets

Dairy Group
2-3 servings

Protein Group
2-3 servings

Vegetable Group
3-5 servings

Fruit Group
2-4 servings

Grain Group 6-11 servings

The Food Guide Pyramid

The food guide pyramid shows six food groups. It tells you how many servings of food you need each day. Your body needs good choices from each group to stay healthy.

Guess What?

The grain group includes bread, cereal, rice, and pasta. You should eat 6 to 11 servings every day.

The Grain Group

Foods at the bottom of the food guide pyramid are made from grains. Grain comes from plant seeds such as oats and wheat. These foods have carbohydrates and fiber. Carbohydrates give your body energy. Fiber helps your body digest food.

digest
to break down food so that it can be used by the body

9

Guess What?

You should eat 3 to 5 servings of vegetables and 2 to 4 servings of fruit every day.

The Fruit and Vegetable Groups

Fruits and vegetables give your body fiber and vitamins. Vitamin C helps your body fight colds. Vitamin A keeps your skin and eyes healthy. Some vegetables also have minerals such as iron and calcium.

mineral
a nutrient found in nature; people need certain minerals to stay healthy.

Guess What?

The dairy group includes cheese, milk, and yogurt. You should eat 2 to 3 servings from the dairy group every day.

The Dairy Group

Foods from the dairy group have calcium, vitamins, and protein. Calcium and vitamin D make your bones and teeth strong. Your body uses protein to make strong muscles.

muscle
a part of the body
that helps it move

13

This part of the pyramid includes beef, chicken, pork, fish, eggs, nuts, and beans. You should eat 2 to 3 servings from the meat and protein group every day.

The Meat and Protein Group

Foods in the meat and protein group come from animals and plants. Meat, fish, nuts, and beans give your body protein and iron. Protein from these foods gives you energy. The right amount of iron helps you stay awake.

Guess What?

The top of the pyramid includes soda, candy, cookies, and chips. You should only eat a small amount of these foods.

Fats, Oils, and Sweets

Fats and oils are found in animals and plants. Your body and brain need a little fat to stay healthy. Sweets have a lot of sugar. Sugar gives you energy for a short time.

Guess What?

Water makes up 3/4 of your body.

Drinking Water

Your body needs water to stay alive. Water carries nutrients to all parts of your body. Water also carries waste out of your body. Drinking water keeps you cool when you sweat. You should drink at least eight glasses of water every day.

Eating Right

Following the food guide pyramid can help you eat right. You should also make good food choices. Choose fruits and vegetables for snacks. Eat less sweets and fatty foods. Your body will get the nutrients it needs when you eat right.

Hands On: Food Diary

The food guide pyramid helps you choose healthy foods. It helps you get all the nutrients that your body needs. You can keep track of what you eat. Does what you eat match the food guide pyramid? You will need seven pieces of paper and a pencil for this activity.

What You Do

1. Put a piece of paper over the food guide pyramid diagram on page 6. Trace the pyramid and draw the lines shown.
2. Repeat step 1 using the other six pieces of paper.
3. Label each piece of paper with a different day of the week.
4. Write down everything you eat inside the pyramid for each day. Make sure to include snacks.
5. Count how many servings of each food group you ate at the end of the day. Keep in mind that some foods contain more than one food group.
6. Look at the food guide pyramid diagram and your food diary at the end of the week. Did you eat enough of each group? Which groups do you need to eat more of? Did you make healthy choices within each group?
7. Try to think of ways you can improve your nutrition.

Words to Know

calcium (KAL-see-uhm)—a soft mineral needed for strong teeth and bones

carbohydrate (kar-boh-HYE-drate)—a nutrient that provides energy

fiber (FYE-bur)—a nutrient that helps your body digest food

iron (EYE-urn)—a mineral that keeps blood healthy and helps people stay awake

mineral (MIN-ur-uhl)—a nutrient found in nature; iron and calcium are minerals.

nutrient (NOO-tree-uhnt)—something that is needed by people, animals, and plants to stay healthy and strong

vitamin (VYE-tuh-min)—a nutrient that helps keep people healthy

Read More

Fisher, Enid. *Food and Health.* Good Health Guides. Milwaukee: Gareth Stevens, 1998.

Royston, Angela. *Eat Well.* Safe and Sound. Des Plaines, Ill.: Heinemann Library, 2000.

Internet Sites

Fresh Starts
http://www.freshstarts.com/home.html
Healthy Eating Club—Games & Quizzes
http://www.healthyeatingclub.com/quizzes-games
Meet the Pyramid Pals
http://www.nutritionexplorations.org/pyramid_cafe/
pc_activities/pyramid_pals.html

Index